PUP CHEF

50 RECIPES YOUR FURRY BEST FRIEND WILL LOVE

Margot Phillips

Legal Notice
The author has made every effort to ensure the accuracy of the information contained in this book. However, the author assumes no liability for errors or omissions.

Disclaimer
Readers should use discretion when introducing new foods or ingredients to their dog's diet, as individual dietary needs and tolerances vary. Always consult your veterinarian before introducing new foods into your dog's diet. Any brand names or trademarks mentioned are the property of their respective owners, and no affiliation or endorsement is implied.

ISBN 979-8-9985038-1-8

DoodleLife Publishing
www.adoodlelife.com
Georgia@adoodlelife.com
Follow us on Instagram @georgiadoodlelife

About the Cover Art

The cover of *Pup Chef: 50 Recipes Your Furry Best Friend Will* Love features a playful, colorful food display based on one of the book's recipes. We highlight the eye-catching Carrot Cheesecake Donuts from page 100, artfully arranged with fresh, dog-friendly ingredients that amplify the design's vibrancy.

The stems and leaves are assembled from celery, with a blueberry positioned at the center of each donut. Teardrop-shaped petals are carefully trimmed from American cheese, providing a soft, golden hue. The butterflies consist of thick-cut turkey for the wings, a thin slice of Colby Cheddar for the body, and shredded carrots for the delicate antennae. The large and small flowers, along with the sun, are formed from layered Colby and Vermont Cheddar, adding depth and texture.

This edible composition sets the tone for the cookbook, reflects its whimsical spirit, and honors the day I brought Georgia home. This cherished photo, taken when she weighed only six pounds, marks the beginning of our story.

Lovingly dedicated to Scott—whose absence is a powerful reminder every single day. Thank you for revealing the beauty of a world shared with dogs. Although our time together was far too short, your presence continues to shape my days and your memory lights my path. I will carry your love in my heart forever.

From Heartbreak to Healing

Certain moments in time can alter your entire course, making you question everything, yet also helping you uncover what truly matters.

Shortly after celebrating the start of 2024 and making plans for our future, my love suddenly passed away. In an instant, my world was turned upside down. The shock of his death left me lost in a void I couldn't escape. I found myself at a crossroads, grieving and unable to imagine what came next. It was during this intense suffering that I decided to invite Georgia into my life.

Georgia, my doodle, will always be far more than a pet—she's my hope and a reminder of love when all else seems to fade. Through her, I've learned that healing can happen in the most unexpected ways. Creating homemade treats began with simply feeding my doodle and grew into a way to foster our bond, turn pain into purpose, and find new meaning. That's how *Pup Chef* was born.

This cookbook isn't just a compilation of recipes—it embodies the love and care I put into each one, as well as the recovery journey we have been through. It represents the deep connection that forms when you nurture your furry best friend and the satisfaction of seeing them flourish with healthy, homemade treats.

While this book is dedicated to Scott—whose memory lives on and guides me—it's also a tribute to Georgia, who taught me that love can be uncovered even in the darkest hours and has the power to transform all things.

Table of Contents

Introduction

Welcome to *Pup Chef: 50 Recipes Your Furry Best Friend Will Love!* If you're anything like me, you want the finest for your furry friend, especially regarding their food. This cookbook celebrates the joy of preparing something special for your pup and the profound bond you share.

As a proud dog mom to Georgia, my lively doodle, and the heart of this book, I have seen firsthand the thrill that comes from homemade treats created with love. My commitment to providing her with delicious, nourishing, and beneficial food motivated me to develop these accessible alternatives using ingredients you likely already have in your kitchen.

Inside, you'll discover an assortment of options for every tail-wagging occasion, from quick snacks and frozen favorites to baked goods and festive delicacies. Whether you're seeking a nutritious daily reward or a fun baking project, this collection makes it easy to pamper your four-legged friend with the quality they deserve.

I hope these recipes bring as much laughter and light to your home as they have to mine. Experiencing Georgia's excitement as she devours these treats is my greatest gift. Here's to more wagging tails, happy tummies, and precious moments with our furry best friends.

Happy Baking!

With love from our kitchen to yours,

Margot

Understanding Ingredients & Nutrition

INGREDIENT SAFETY & SENSITIVITIES

Every dog is unique—what works for one pup may not be right for another. Some dogs have allergies or intolerances, so it's important to introduce new components slowly and observe their reactions. Always adhere to safe guidelines and consult your vet if you're unsure about presenting unfamiliar foods. Just because an ingredient is acceptable for dogs does not mean it will agree with yours. For example, many dogs can tolerate dairy, while others might face digestive issues. The same is true for gluten—some dogs can handle it, while others may be sensitive. Numerous recipes in this book are dairy-free and gluten-free, but a few include yogurt, cheese, or gluten-containing ingredients. Recipes marked with these stars indicate those that are dairy-free and gluten-free.

GF DF

UNDERSTANDING YOUR DOG'S DIETARY NEEDS

Dogs thrive on a well-rounded diet that offers a range of protein-rich foods, healthy fats, and carbohydrate-dense whole foods. Although these recipes are intended as treats rather than complete servings, they contribute vital nutrients that complement your pup's eating habits. Snacks should account for only a minor part of their overall nutrition, while main meals should deliver the fundamental vitamins and minerals. For more details, refer to the ingredient benefit section, which explains how different items support your dog's wellness.

CHOOSING HIGH-QUALITY INGREDIENTS

Fresh, natural, and minimally processed foods are the top choices for your pup's health. Select organic or locally sourced produce whenever possible to ensure purity and avoid unnecessary additives. Additionally, it is wise to integrate single-ingredient foods, such as lean meats, fruits, and vegetables, into their diet.

FOODS THAT YOU SHOULD NEVER GIVE YOUR DOG

Although countless foods are suitable for human consumption, many can be poisonous to dogs, resulting in serious or potentially fatal health issues. Avoiding these harmful foods is crucial for protecting your dog's safety and overall well-being.

Alcohol can cause vomiting, diarrhea, breathing issues, and notable toxicity.

Artificial sweeteners, particularly xylitol, may lead to a rapid drop in blood sugar and potential liver failure.

Avocados contain persin, which can be toxic to dogs.

Chocolate and **cocoa powder** contain theobromine, which is toxic to dogs.

Currants, grapes, and raisins, even in minimal quantities, can lead to kidney failure.

Garlic and **onions** can damage red blood cells, resulting in anemia.

Lemons and limes contain citric acid and essential oils, which may cause digestive upset.

Macadamia nuts may trigger symptoms such as tremors, vomiting, and weakness.

Wild mushrooms or **unidentified varieties** can be toxic and result in organ failure.

Pecans and walnuts contain high levels of toxins that can impact the nervous system.

Excess **salt** can result in sodium ion poisoning and dehydration.

Yeast dough can expand in the stomach, leading to bloating and possibly resulting in a rupture.

Special Tools

Many recipes in this book utilize standard kitchen essentials, such as baking sheets, mixing bowls, spatulas, parchment paper, measuring cups, and a rolling pin. However, incorporating a few additional tools can simplify the process. These suggested items will help construct well-shaped treats, improve efficiency, and elevate your baking activity. With the proper equipment, your pup's treats will turn out wonderfully.

Silicone popsicle molds & wooden sticks
Form delightful frozen treats.
(12 cavities)

Silicone mini muffin or mini cupcake pans
Create small bite-sized muffins or cupcakes.
(24 cavities)

Silicone mini donut pans
Produce consistent, donut-shaped treats with ease.
(24 cavities)

Cookie cutters
Shape biscuits and baked goods into fun, uniform designs.
(Small & medium sizes)

Blender or food processor
Purees fruits and vegetables into a smooth mixture.

Cookie stamps
Add decorative imprints to cookies, providing a professional touch.

Semi-automatic stainless-steel whisk, hand mixer
Speeds up mixing batters, frostings, and icings for a silky, well-incorporated texture.

Healthy Fruit & Veggie Snacks

Fruits and vegetables make fantastic low-calorie snacks. They are rich in fiber, vitamins, and antioxidants. Always wash produce thoroughly, remove seeds and cores when needed, and peel when necessary. Feed them in moderation, accounting for no more than 10% of your dog's daily diet. Avoid adding oils, seasonings, and salt. Hard vegetables may need to be steamed or boiled to aid digestion, while softer types can typically be offered raw.

Apples
Wash well. Remove the core and seeds, then cut into thin slices.

Bananas
Peel the skin. Mash or slice into bite-sized pieces.

Blackberries
Wash gently. Serve whole or halved. Feed in moderation due to natural sugar and fiber.

Blueberries
Wash gently. Serve whole or halved, fresh or thawed from frozen.

Cantaloupes
Wash well. Cut in half lengthwise and scoop out the seeds. Slice or cube the flesh.

Butternut Squash
Peel the skin, remove the seeds, and cut into bite-sized cubes. Steam, boil, or bake until tender.

Oranges
Peel, remove the seeds, and separate into segments. Feed in moderation due to high acidity and sugar.

Watermelon
Remove rind and seeds, as they can cause digestive issues. Cut into cubes. Feed in moderation due to high sugar.

Pears
Wash well. Remove the core, seeds, and stem, then cut into small pieces.

Kiwis
Wash well. Peel the skin and cut into small pieces.

Plums
Wash well. Remove the pit and cut into small pieces. Avoid canned plums that contain added sugar.

Pineapples
Wash well. Remove the skin and core. Cut into bite-sized pieces.

Peaches
Wash well. Remove the pit and slice into small pieces. Avoid canned peaches with added sugar.

Raspberries
Wash gently. Serve whole or halved. Feed in moderation due to natural sugar and fiber content.

Strawberries
Wash well. Remove stems and slice or serve whole. Serve in moderation due to natural sugars.

Mangos
Wash well. Peel the skin, remove the pit, and cut into small cubes. Feed in moderation due to high sugar.

Asparagus
Wash and remove tough ends. Steam or lightly boil until tender. Cut into bite-sized pieces.

Carrots
Wash, peel, and slice into sticks or rounds. Steam, boil or serve raw.

Cabbage
Wash well and remove the outer leaves. Chop into small, bite-sized pieces. Steam or lightly boil for easier digestion.

Brussels Sprouts
Wash well and trim ends. Serve steamed or boiled.

Bell Peppers
Wash, remove the seeds, and the stem. Cut into slices or small pieces. Serve raw or lightly cooked.

Sweet Potatoes
Wash well. Peel and cut into bite-sized cubes. Steam, boil, or bake until tender. Then mash or serve cubed.

Green Beans
Wash well. Steam, lightly boil, or serve raw. Cut into bite-sized pieces.

Celery
Wash well and cut into small sticks or bite-sized pieces. Best served raw.

Cauliflower
Wash and separate into small florets. Steam or boil until tender.

Cucumbers
Wash and peel the skin. Slice into rounds or sticks. Best served raw. Use seedless varieties, as seeds may cause digestive issues.

Spinach
Wash well. Steam or lightly sauté, then chop for easy serving.

Pumpkin
Remove seeds and skin. Cut into bite-sized cubes. Steam or bake until tender. Then mash or serve cubed.

Broccoli Florets
Wash and separate into small florets. Steam or boil until tender. Avoid stems, as they may be difficult to digest.

Zucchini
Wash well and slice into rounds or sticks. Serve raw, steamed, or boiled.

Tasty Treats

Apple Berry Mini Cakes

Approximately 24 mini cakes

INGREDIENTS

¼ cup (37g) fresh blueberries, sliced in half
½ cup (125g) unsweetened applesauce
½ cup (83g) strawberries, diced (remove green tops)
1 egg
1 cup (90g) oat flour

SPECIAL TOOLS

24-cavity mini silicone cupcake pans

GF DF

DIRECTIONS

1. Preheat the oven to 350°F (180°C). Use mini silicone cupcake pans or lightly coat non-silicone pans with nonstick baking spray.
2. In a medium bowl, mix the sliced blueberries, applesauce, diced strawberries, egg, and oat flour until well combined.
3. If using silicone, spoon the batter directly into the pans, filling completely. For non-silicone pans, fill each about three-quarters full.
4. Bake for 15–20 minutes or until a toothpick inserted into the center comes out clean. Let the cakes cool in the pan for 5 minutes, then carefully unmold and transfer them to a wire rack to cool completely before serving.
5. Store in an airtight container in the fridge for up to 5 days.

Apple Peanut Butter Treats

Approximately 25–30 treats

INGREDIENTS

1 cup (250g) unsweetened applesauce
1 large egg
½ cup (128g) unsweetened creamy peanut butter (xylitol-free)
½ teaspoon plain cinnamon
2 cups (240g) whole wheat flour

SPECIAL TOOLS

flower-shape cookie cutter

DF

DIRECTIONS

1. Preheat the oven to 350°F (180°C) and line a baking sheet with parchment paper.
2. In a medium bowl, mix the applesauce, egg, peanut butter, cinnamon, and whole wheat flour thoroughly until a dough forms. If the dough is too sticky, add extra flour.
3. Using a rolling pin, roll the dough on a lightly floured surface to a thickness of one-quarter inch. (See how to roll out dough on page 113.) Then, cut out shapes with a cookie cutter and arrange the cutouts on the prepared baking sheet.
4. Bake for 12–15 minutes or until firm to the touch and golden brown. Cool completely before serving.
5. Store in an airtight container in the fridge for up to 7 days.

Banana Beet Treats

Approximately 20 treats

INGREDIENTS

1 ripe banana

1 fresh beet, either steamed, roasted, or pre-packaged

2 cups (180g) oat flour

SPECIAL TOOLS

heart-shape cookie cutter

GF DF

DIRECTIONS

1. Preheat the oven to 350°F (180°C) and line a baking sheet with parchment paper.

- Divide the ingredients in half to make two separate doughs.

2. In a small bowl, mash the banana until it's smooth. Add 1 tablespoon of water and stir in 1 cup of oat flour until well combined. Set aside.
3. Using a blender, mash the beet with 2 tablespoons of water until smooth. Then, pour the mixture into a small bowl and add 1 cup of oat flour, stirring until well combined. If the mixture is too sticky, add more flour; if it's too crumbly, add more water.
4. Using a rolling pin, roll each dough piece by itself on a lightly floured surface to a thickness of one-quarter inch. (See how to roll out dough on page 113.) Place one rolled dough on top of the other and cut layered shapes with a cookie cutter. Then, arrange the layered hearts as single treats on the prepared baking sheet.
5. Bake for 15–18 minutes or until golden and set. Cool completely before serving.
6. Store in an airtight container in the fridge for up to 5 days.

Banana Coconut Drops

Approximately 12–15 drops

INGREDIENTS

½ cup (120g) ripe banana, mashed
¼ cup (24g) unsweetened shredded coconut
1 egg
1 cup (90g) oat flour

GF DF

DIRECTIONS

1. Preheat the oven to 350°F (180°C) and line a baking sheet with parchment paper.
2. In a medium bowl, mash the banana until it's smooth. Add the shredded coconut, egg, and oat flour, mixing until thoroughly combined.
3. Scoop out tablespoon-sized portions and roll them into rounds with your hands. Arrange the rounds on the prepared baking sheet, spacing them an inch apart.
4. Bake for 10–12 minutes or until firm to the touch. Cool completely before serving.
5. Store in an airtight container in the fridge for up to 7 days.

Banana Crunch Bites

Approximately 8–10 bites

INGREDIENTS

1 large ripe banana

1½ cups (144g) rolled oats

3 tablespoons pure honey

4 tablespoons melted coconut oil, divided

GF DF

DIRECTIONS

1. Preheat the oven to 325°F (165°C) and line a small baking sheet with parchment paper. Ensure the baking sheet fits in the fridge.
2. In a medium bowl, mix the rolled oats, honey, and 2 tablespoons of melted coconut oil until well blended. Spread the mixture on the prepared baking sheet.
3. Bake for 12–15 minutes or until golden brown. Let it cool, then measure ½ cup of toasted oats into a bowl for rolling and set it aside.
4. In a medium bowl, mash the banana until it's smooth. Add the remaining toasted oats and coconut oil, mixing until well combined.
5. Scoop out 2 tablespoon-sized portions and roll them into rounds with your hands. Then, coat each one in the reserved toasted oats, ensuring it is fully covered.
6. Return the coated rounds to the parchment-lined baking sheet and refrigerate for 1 hour before serving.
7. Store in an airtight container in the fridge for up to 5 days.

Beef Blueberry Meatballs

Approximately 10-15 meatballs

INGREDIENTS

½ cup (113g) 90% lean ground beef, raw
½ cup (74g) fresh blueberries, sliced in half
1 egg
1 cup (90g) oat flour
1-2 tablespoons of water or unsweetened coconut milk, if needed for moisture

GF DF

DIRECTIONS

1. Preheat the oven to 350°F (180°C) and line a baking sheet with parchment paper.
2. In a medium bowl, mix the raw ground beef, sliced blueberries, egg, and oat flour until well combined. If the mixture is too dry, add coconut milk or water as needed.
3. Scoop out tablespoon-sized portions and roll them into rounds with your hands. Arrange the rounds on the prepared baking sheet, spacing them an inch apart.
4. Bake for 20-25 minutes, or until fully cooked and the internal temperature reaches 160°F (71°C). Cool completely before serving.
5. Store in an airtight container in the fridge for up to 5 days.

Beef Spinach Minis

Approximately 24 minis

INGREDIENTS

1 lb (454g) 90% lean ground beef, raw
½ cup (15g) spinach, chopped
1 egg
1¼ cups (113g) oat flour

GF DF

DIRECTIONS

1. Preheat the oven to 350°F (180°C) and line a baking sheet with parchment paper.
2. In a medium bowl, mix the raw ground beef, egg, chopped spinach, and oat flour until well combined.
3. Scoop out tablespoon-sized portions and roll them into rounds with your hands. Arrange the rounds on the prepared baking sheet, spacing them an inch apart.
4. Bake for 18–20 minutes, or until fully cooked and the internal temperature reaches 160°F (71°C). Cool completely before serving.
5. Store in an airtight container in the fridge for up to 5 days.

Berrylicious Oat Squares

Approximately 20 squares

INGREDIENTS

¼ cup (63g) unsweetened applesauce

1 egg

¼ cup (42g) fresh strawberries, mashed (remove green tops)

¼ cup (37g) fresh blueberries, sliced in half

1 cup (96g) rolled oats

GF DF

DIRECTIONS

1. Preheat the oven to 350°F (180°C) and coat a 7x7-inch baking pan with nonstick baking spray.
2. In a medium bowl, mix the applesauce, egg, mashed strawberries, sliced blueberries, and rolled oats until well combined.
3. Spread the mixture with a spatula into the prepared baking pan, smoothing it into an even layer, pressing down gently to flatten.
4. Bake for 20–25 minutes or until the center is set and the edges are firm. Cool completely in the pan, then cut into small squares and serve.
5. Store in an airtight container in the fridge for up to 5 days.

Carrot Apple Muffins

Approximately 24 mini muffins

INGREDIENTS

½ cup (55g) carrots, grated
½ cup (64g) apple, grated (remove seeds and core)
1 cup (96g) rolled oats
¼ cup (63g) unsweetened applesauce
1 egg
1 teaspoon baking powder
¼ cup (23g) oat flour

SPECIAL TOOLS

24-cavity mini silicone muffin pans

GF DF

DIRECTIONS

1. Preheat the oven to 375°F (190°C). Use mini silicone muffin pans or coat non-silicone pans with nonstick baking spray.
2. In a large bowl, mix the grated carrots, rolled oats, grated apple, applesauce, egg, baking powder, and oat flour until well combined.
3. If using silicone, spoon the batter directly into the pans, filling completely. For non-silicone pans, fill each about three-quarters full.
4. Bake for 20–25 minutes or until a toothpick inserted into the center comes out clean. Let the muffins cool in the pan for 5 minutes, then carefully unmold and transfer them to a wire rack to cool completely before serving.
5. Store in an airtight container in the fridge for up to 5 days.

Carrot Peanut Butter Biscuits

Approximately 18–24 biscuits

INGREDIENTS

½ cup (128g) unsweetened creamy peanut butter (xylitol-free)
1 cup (110g) carrots, grated
1 egg
1 cup (90g) oat flour
¼ cup water, if needed for moisture

SPECIAL TOOLS

smiley-face cookie stamp & round cookie cutter

GF DF

DIRECTIONS

1. Preheat the oven to 350°F (180°C) and line a baking sheet with parchment paper.
2. In a medium bowl, mix the peanut butter, egg, grated carrots, and oat flour thoroughly until a dough forms. If the mixture is too dry, add water one tablespoon at a time.
3. Scoop out 1½ tablespoon-sized portions and roll them into rounds with your hands. Gently flatten each one, press with a cookie stamp, and trim with a round cookie cutter. (See how to use a cookie stamp on page 113.) Arrange them on the prepared baking sheet, spacing them an inch apart.
4. Bake for 25–30 minutes or until the edges are firm and lightly golden. Cool completely before serving.
5. Store in an airtight container in the fridge for up to 7 days.

Cheese Sticks

Approximately 12–14 sticks

INGREDIENTS

½ cup (56g) low-sodium shredded cheddar cheese, plus ¼ cup (28g) for sprinkling
2 large eggs, divided
¼ cup (63g) unsweetened applesauce
1½ cups (180g) whole wheat flour

DIRECTIONS

1. Preheat the oven to 375°F (190°C).
2. In a small bowl, beat 1 egg and set it aside for the egg wash. In a medium bowl, mix the ½ cup shredded cheddar cheese, applesauce, the remaining egg, and whole wheat flour thoroughly until a dough forms.
3. Using a rolling pin, roll the dough on lightly floured parchment paper into a 6x12-inch rectangle. Brush with the egg wash and sprinkle half of the reserved cheese on top. Cover with a second piece of parchment, flip, and repeat on the other side with the remaining cheese. Cut into 1½-inch strips, twist, and arrange the sticks on the parchment-lined baking sheet.
4. Bake for 16–20 minutes or until crispy and golden brown. Gently separate pieces that are stuck together. Cool completely before serving.
5. Store in an airtight container in the fridge for up to 5 days.

Cheesy Chicken Meatballs

Approximately 15–20 meatballs

INGREDIENTS

1 lb (454g) boneless, skinless chicken breast,
raw and ground
½ cup (41g) broccoli, finely chopped, steamed or raw
2 tablespoons canned unsweetened pumpkin purée
¼ cup (28g) low-sodium shredded cheddar cheese

GF

DIRECTIONS

1. Preheat the oven to 350°F (180°C) and line a baking sheet with parchment paper.
2. Grind the raw, boneless chicken breast until it reaches a ground consistency. (See how to grind chicken on page 112.) In a large bowl, mix the pumpkin purée, raw ground chicken, chopped broccoli, and cheddar cheese, until well blended.
3. Scoop out tablespoon-sized portions and roll them into rounds with your hands. Arrange the rounds on the prepared baking sheet, spacing them an inch apart.
4. Bake for 20–25 minutes, or until fully cooked and the internal temperature reaches 165°F (74°C). Cool completely before serving.
5. Store in an airtight container in the fridge for up to 5 days.

Cheesy Spinach Treats

Approximately 15–20 treats

INGREDIENTS

1 cup (30g) spinach, chopped
½ cup (56g) low-sodium shredded cheddar cheese
1 egg
¼ cup water
1 cup (120g) whole wheat flour, plus more for dusting

SPECIAL TOOLS

flower-shape cookie cutter

DIRECTIONS

1. Preheat the oven to 350°F (180°C) and line a baking sheet with parchment paper.
2. In a medium bowl, mix the chopped spinach, shredded cheddar cheese, egg, water, and whole wheat flour thoroughly until a dough forms.
3. Using a rolling pin, roll the dough on a lightly floured surface to a thickness of one-quarter inch. (See how to roll out dough on page 113.) Then, cut out shapes with a cookie cutter and arrange the cutouts on the prepared baking sheet.
4. Bake for 20–25 minutes or until firm to the touch. Cool completely before serving.
5. Store in an airtight container in the fridge for up to 5 days.

Coconut Pumpkin Treats

Approximately 15–20 treats

INGREDIENTS

¼ cup (24g) unsweetened shredded coconut
½ cup (122g) canned unsweetened pumpkin purée
1 egg
1¾ cups (158g) oat flour

SPECIAL TOOLS

heart-shape cookie cutter

GF DF

DIRECTIONS

1. Preheat the oven to 350°F (180°C) and line a baking sheet with parchment paper.
2. In a medium bowl, mix the shredded coconut, pumpkin purée, egg, and oat flour thoroughly until a dough forms.
3. Using a rolling pin, roll the dough on a lightly floured surface to a thickness of one-quarter inch. (See how to roll out dough on page 113.) Then, cut out shapes with a cookie cutter and arrange the cutouts on the prepared baking sheet.
4. Bake for 12–15 minutes or until firm to the touch and golden brown. Cool completely before serving.
5. Store in an airtight container in the fridge for up to 7 days.

Cranberry Beef Cookies

Approximately 15–20 cookies

INGREDIENTS

1 lb (454g) 90% lean ground beef, raw
½ cup (50g) fresh cranberries, chopped
1 egg
1 cup (90g) oat flour

GF DF

DIRECTIONS

1. Preheat the oven to 350°F (180°C) and line a baking sheet with parchment paper.
2. In a medium bowl, mix the raw ground beef, chopped cranberries, egg, and oat flour until thoroughly combined.
3. Scoop out tablespoon-sized portions and roll them into rounds with your hands. Arrange the rounds on the prepared baking sheet, spacing them an inch apart. Then, press the bottom of a glass on each round to flatten it slightly.
4. Bake for 18–20 minutes, or until fully cooked and the internal temperature reaches 160°F (71°C). Cool completely before serving.
5. Store in an airtight container in the fridge for up to 5 days.

Georgia's Fruit Bars

Approximately 12-16 small bars

INGREDIENTS

1 ripe banana, mashed
½ cup (74g) fresh blueberries, sliced in half
¼ cup (32g) apple, grated (remove seeds and core)
½ cup (125g) unsweetened applesauce
1 tablespoon pure honey
1 egg
1 cup (96g) rolled oats

GF DF

DIRECTIONS

1. Preheat the oven to 350°F (180°C) and coat a 9x9-inch baking pan with nonstick baking spray.
2. In a medium bowl, mash the banana until it's smooth. Combine the sliced blueberries, egg, applesauce, grated apple, honey, and rolled oats, mixing until well blended.
3. Spread the mixture with a spatula into the prepared baking pan, smoothing it into an even layer, pressing down gently to flatten.
4. Bake for 30-35 minutes, or until the center is set and the edges are firm. Cool completely in the pan, then cut into small squares and serve.
5. Store in an airtight container in the fridge for up to 5 days.

Harvest Carob Cookies

Approximately 24 cookies

INGREDIENTS

¼ cup (64g) unsweetened almond butter
¼ cup (64g) unsweetened creamy peanut butter (xylitol-free)
1 cup (244g) canned unsweetened pumpkin purée
2 large eggs
1 cup (112g) almond flour
1½ cups (135g) oat flour, plus more for dusting

GLAZE

⅓ cup (75g) carob chips
1 tablespoon olive oil

SPECIAL TOOLS

flower-shape cookie cutter

GF DF

DIRECTIONS

1. Preheat the oven to 350°F (180°C) and line a baking sheet with parchment paper. Then, place a wire rack over another sheet.
2. In a large bowl, combine the almond butter, peanut butter, eggs, and pumpkin purée until smooth and well blended. Gradually fold in the oat flour and almond flour, stirring until a dough forms.
3. Using a rolling pin, roll the dough on a lightly floured surface to a thickness of one-quarter inch. (See how to roll out dough on page 113.) Then, cut out shapes with a cookie cutter and arrange the cutouts on the prepared baking sheet.
4. Bake for 25–30 minutes or until firm to the touch and golden brown. Let the cookies cool on the baking sheet for 5 minutes, then carefully transfer them to the wire rack to cool completely before glazing.
5. **Make the glaze:** Melt carob chips and olive oil in a double boiler, stirring until smooth. (See how to melt carob on page 113.)
6. Drizzle the glaze over the cooled cookies on the wire rack, letting the excess drip onto the parchment paper. Allow the glaze to set before serving or storing.
7. Store in an airtight container in the fridge for up to 5 days.

Oat Peanut Butter Cookies

Approximately 25–30 cookies

INGREDIENTS

2 tablespoons unsweetened applesauce
½ cup (128g) unsweetened creamy peanut butter (xylitol-free)
1 egg
¾ cup (68g) oat flour

GF DF

DIRECTIONS

1. Preheat the oven to 350°F (180°C) and line a baking sheet with parchment paper.
2. In a medium bowl, mix the applesauce, egg, peanut butter, and oat flour until thoroughly combined.
3. Scoop out tablespoon-sized portions and roll them into rounds with your hands. Arrange the rounds on the prepared baking sheet, spacing them an inch apart. Flatten each with a fork to create a crosshatch pattern.
4. Bake for 15–17 minutes or until the edges are lightly golden. Cool completely before serving.
5. Store in an airtight container in the fridge for up to 7 days.

Peach Banana Pupcakes

Approximately 24 pupcakes

INGREDIENTS

1 ripe banana, mashed

½ cup (77g) fresh peach, finely diced (pit removed)

1 egg

1 cup (90g) oat flour

SPECIAL TOOLS

24-cavity mini silicone cupcake pans

GF DF

DIRECTIONS

1. Preheat the oven to 325°F (165°C). Use mini silicone cupcake pans or lightly coat non-silicone pans with nonstick baking spray.
2. In a medium bowl, mash the banana until it's smooth. Add the diced peach, egg, and oat flour, mixing until well combined.
3. If using silicone, spoon the batter directly into the pans, filling completely. For non-silicone pans, fill each about three-quarters full.
4. Bake for 25–30 minutes or until a toothpick inserted into the center comes out clean. Let the cakes cool in the pan for 5 minutes, then carefully unmold and transfer them to a wire rack to cool completely before serving.
5. Store in an airtight container in the fridge for up to 5 days.

Peanut Butter & Banana Bites

Approximately 15–20 bites

INGREDIENTS

2 ripe bananas, mashed
½ cup (128g) unsweetened creamy peanut butter (xylitol-free)
1 cup (96g) rolled oats
¼ teaspoon cinnamon

GF DF

DIRECTIONS

1. Preheat the oven to 350°F (180°C) and line a baking sheet with parchment paper.
2. In a medium bowl, mash the bananas until smooth. Add the peanut butter, rolled oats, and cinnamon, mixing until well combined.
3. Scoop out tablespoon-sized portions and roll them into rounds with your hands. Arrange the rounds on the prepared baking sheet, spacing them an inch apart. Then, flatten each slightly with the back of a spoon.
4. Bake for 15–17 minutes or until firm. Cool completely before serving.
5. Store in an airtight container in the fridge for up to 5 days.

Pear Banana Squares

Approximately 20 squares

INGREDIENTS

½ cup (77g) fresh pear, finely diced (seeds and core removed)
½ ripe banana, mashed
¼ cup (63g) unsweetened applesauce
1 egg
2 cups (180g) oat flour

GF DF

DIRECTIONS

1. Preheat the oven to 325°F (165°C) and coat a 9x6-inch baking pan with nonstick baking spray.
2. In a medium bowl, mash the banana until it's smooth. Add the egg, pear, applesauce, and oat flour, mixing until well combined.
3. Spread the mixture with a spatula into the prepared baking pan, smoothing it into an even layer, pressing down firmly to flatten.
4. Bake for 30–35 minutes, or until a toothpick inserted into the center comes out clean and the edges are firm. Cool completely in the pan, then cut into small squares and serve.
5. Store in an airtight container in the fridge for up to 5 days.

Pumpkin Chews

Approximately 18–25 chews

INGREDIENTS

1½ cups (144g) rolled oats
1 cup (244g) canned unsweetened pumpkin purée
1 egg
1 tablespoon pure honey

GF DF

DIRECTIONS

1. Preheat the oven to 350°F (180°C) and line a baking sheet with parchment paper.
2. In a medium bowl, mix the pumpkin purée, rolled oats, egg, and honey until thoroughly combined.
3. Scoop out tablespoon-sized portions and roll them into rounds with your hands. Arrange the rounds on the prepared baking sheet, spacing them an inch apart. Then, flatten each slightly with the back of a spoon.
4. Bake for 20–25 minutes or until the edges are lightly golden and firm to the touch. Cool completely before serving.
5. Store in an airtight container in the fridge for up to 5 days.

Pumpkin Peanut Butter Treats

Approximately 25–30 treats

INGREDIENTS

½ cup (128g) unsweetened creamy peanut butter (xylitol-free)
1 cup (244g) canned unsweetened pumpkin purée
½ teaspoon cinnamon
1¾ cups (210g) whole wheat flour

SPECIAL TOOLS

large star-shape cookie cutter

DF

DIRECTIONS

1. Preheat the oven to 350°F (180°C) and line a baking sheet with parchment paper.
2. In a medium bowl, mix the pumpkin purée, peanut butter, and cinnamon until smooth. Gradually add the whole wheat flour, stirring until a dough forms.
3. Using a rolling pin, roll the dough on a lightly floured surface to a thickness of one-quarter inch. (See how to roll out dough on page 113.) Then, cut out shapes with a cookie cutter and arrange the cutouts on the prepared baking sheet.
4. Bake for 20–25 minutes or until firm to the touch and golden brown. Cool completely before serving.
5. Store in an airtight container in the fridge for up to 5 days.

Sweet Honey Squares

Approximately 20-25 squares

INGREDIENTS

¼ cup (63g) unsweetened applesauce
1 cup (96g) rolled oats
1 tablespoon pure honey
1 egg
½ cup (45g) oat flour

GF DF

DIRECTIONS

1. Preheat the oven to 350°F (180°C) and coat a 9x6-inch baking pan with nonstick baking spray.
2. In a medium bowl, mix the applesauce, egg, honey, rolled oats, and oat flour until well combined.
3. Spread the mixture with a spatula into the prepared baking pan, smoothing it into an even layer, pressing down firmly to flatten.
4. Bake for 15–20 minutes or until the edges are firm and golden brown. Cool completely in the pan, then cut into small squares and serve.
5. Store in an airtight container in the fridge for up to 5 days.

Toasted Coconut Peanut Nibbles

Approximately 12 nibbles

INGREDIENTS

½ cup (48g) unsweetened shredded coconut
2 tablespoons unsweetened almond butter
½ cup (128g) unsweetened creamy peanut butter (xylitol-free)
1 tablespoon pure honey
¾ cup (68g) oat flour

GF DF

DIRECTIONS

1. Preheat the oven to 325°F (165°C) and line a small baking sheet with parchment paper. Ensure the baking sheet fits in the fridge.
2. Spread the shredded coconut evenly on the prepared baking sheet. Bake for 6–8 minutes, stirring every 2 minutes, until it becomes light golden brown. Watch closely, as it can burn quickly. Once toasted, transfer the coconut to a shallow bowl and set aside.
3. In a medium bowl, combine the almond and peanut butter with the honey and oat flour, mixing until thoroughly blended.
4. Scoop out 1½ tablespoon-sized portions and roll them into rounds with your hands. Coat each round in the toasted coconut until fully covered.
5. Place the coated rounds on the parchment-lined baking sheet and refrigerate for 1 hour before serving.
6. Store in an airtight container in the fridge for up to 5 days.

BAKED WITH LOVE
BAKED WITH LOVE
BAKED WITH LOVE
BAKED WITH LOVE
BAKED WITH LOVE
BAKED WITH LOVE
BAKED WITH LOVE
BAKED WITH LOVE

Tropical Fruit Biscuits

Approximately 15–20 biscuits

INGREDIENTS

¼ cup (60g) ripe banana, mashed
1 tablespoon unsweetened shredded coconut
¼ cup (42g) fresh pineapple, chopped
1 egg
1 cup (90g) oat flour

SPECIAL TOOLS

cookie stamp & round cookie cutter

GF DF

DIRECTIONS

1. Preheat the oven to 350°F (180°C) and line a baking sheet with parchment paper.
2. In a medium bowl, mash the banana until it's smooth. Add the shredded coconut, chopped pineapple, egg, and oat flour, mixing until thoroughly combined.
3. Scoop out 1½ tablespoon-sized portions and roll them into rounds with your hands. Gently flatten each one, press with a cookie stamp, and trim with a round cookie cutter. (See how to use a cookie stamp on page 113.) Arrange them on the prepared baking sheet, spacing them an inch apart.
4. Bake for 20–25 minutes or until lightly golden and firm. Cool completely before serving.
5. Store in an airtight container in the fridge for up to 7 days.

Turkey Sweet Potato Treats

Approximately 25–30 treats

INGREDIENTS

2 strips of turkey bacon, cooked and finely chopped
1 lb (454g) 93% lean ground turkey, cooked
1 cup (240g) sweet potatoes, mashed and cooked
2 eggs, lightly beaten
½ cup (60g) coconut flour
½ cup low-sodium chicken broth or water, adjust as needed for consistency

GF DF

DIRECTIONS

1. In a nonstick skillet, brown the ground turkey over medium heat until it reaches an internal temperature of 165°F (74°C). Allow it to cool slightly, then set it aside. In a separate skillet, cook the turkey bacon until crispy. Break it into small pieces, let it cool a bit, and set it aside. Meanwhile, peel and dice the sweet potato into small cubes, then boil for 10–15 minutes until tender. Afterward, mash it and let it cool slightly before using.
2. Preheat the oven to 350°F (180°C) and line a baking sheet with parchment paper.
3. In a large bowl, mix the cooked turkey and cooked turkey bacon with the eggs, mashed sweet potatoes, and coconut flour until well blended. Gradually add the chicken broth or water until the mixture holds together without becoming too sticky.
4. Scoop out tablespoon-sized portions and roll them into rounds with your hands. Arrange the rounds on the prepared baking sheet, spacing them an inch apart.
5. Bake for 20–25 minutes or until lightly golden and firm. Cool completely before serving.
6. Store in an airtight container in the fridge for up to 5 days.

Zucchini Cheese Muffins

Approximately 24 mini muffins

INGREDIENTS

1 cup (112g) low-sodium shredded cheddar cheese
1 cup (124g) zucchini, grated
1 large egg
1 cup (90g) oat flour
¼ cup water, if needed for moisture

SPECIAL TOOLS

24-cavity mini silicone muffin pans

GF

DIRECTIONS

1. Preheat the oven to 350°F (180°C). Use mini silicone muffin pans or coat non-silicone pans with nonstick baking spray.
2. In a large bowl, thoroughly mix the shredded cheese, egg, and grated zucchini. Gradually add the oat flour, stirring until just blended. If the mixture is too dry, add water 1 tablespoon at a time.
3. If using silicone, spoon the batter directly into the pans, filling completely. For non-silicone pans, fill each about three-quarters full.
4. Bake for 20–25 minutes or until a toothpick inserted into the center comes out clean. Let the muffins cool in the pan for 5 minutes, then carefully unmold and transfer them to a wire rack to cool completely before serving.
5. Store in an airtight container in the fridge for up to 5 days.

One-Ingredient Healthy Bites

Apple Chips

INGREDIENTS

1–2 large apples

GF DF

DIRECTIONS

1. Preheat the oven to 200°F (95°C) and line a baking sheet with parchment paper.
2. Wash the apple and remove the seeds and core. Cut into thin slices and arrange them in a single layer on the prepared baking sheet.
3. Bake for 2–3 hours, or until fully dried and crisp. Cool completely before serving.
4. Store in an airtight container in the fridge for up to 14 days.

Banana Chips

INGREDIENTS

1–2 ripe bananas

coconut oil spray (optional)

GF DF

DIRECTIONS

1. Preheat the oven to 250°F (120°C) and line a baking sheet with parchment paper.
2. Slice the bananas into thin, even rounds and arrange them in a single layer on the baking sheet.
3. For extra crispiness, lightly spray both sides of the banana slices with coconut oil.
4. Bake for 1½–2 hours, flipping halfway or until fully dried and crisp. Cool completely before serving.
5. Store in an airtight container in the fridge for up to 14 days.

Pumpkin Bites

INGREDIENTS

Select the Pumpkin. Use a sugar or pie pumpkin for the best taste and texture. Avoid large carving pumpkins—they tend to be watery and less flavorful.

GF DF

DIRECTIONS

1. Preheat the oven to 375°F (190°C) and line a baking sheet with parchment paper.
2. Begin by thoroughly washing the pumpkin. Cut in half and remove the seeds along with the stringy insides. Use a vegetable peeler or a sharp knife to remove the skin. Cut the flesh into bite-sized cubes and arrange in a single layer on the prepared baking sheet.
3. Bake for 20–25 minutes, or until tender when pierced with a fork. Cool completely before serving.
4. Store in an airtight container in the fridge for up to 5 days or freeze for up to 2 months.

Sweet Potato Chews

Approximately 6–8 chews

INGREDIENTS

1 large sweet potato

GF DF

DIRECTIONS

1. Preheat the oven to 250°F (120°C) and line a baking sheet with parchment paper.
2. Wash and peel the sweet potato. Thinly slice into long strips and arrange them in a single layer on the prepared baking sheet.
3. Bake for 2½–3 hours, flipping halfway, or until fully dried and chewy. Cool completely before serving.
4. Store in an airtight container in the fridge for up to 7 days.

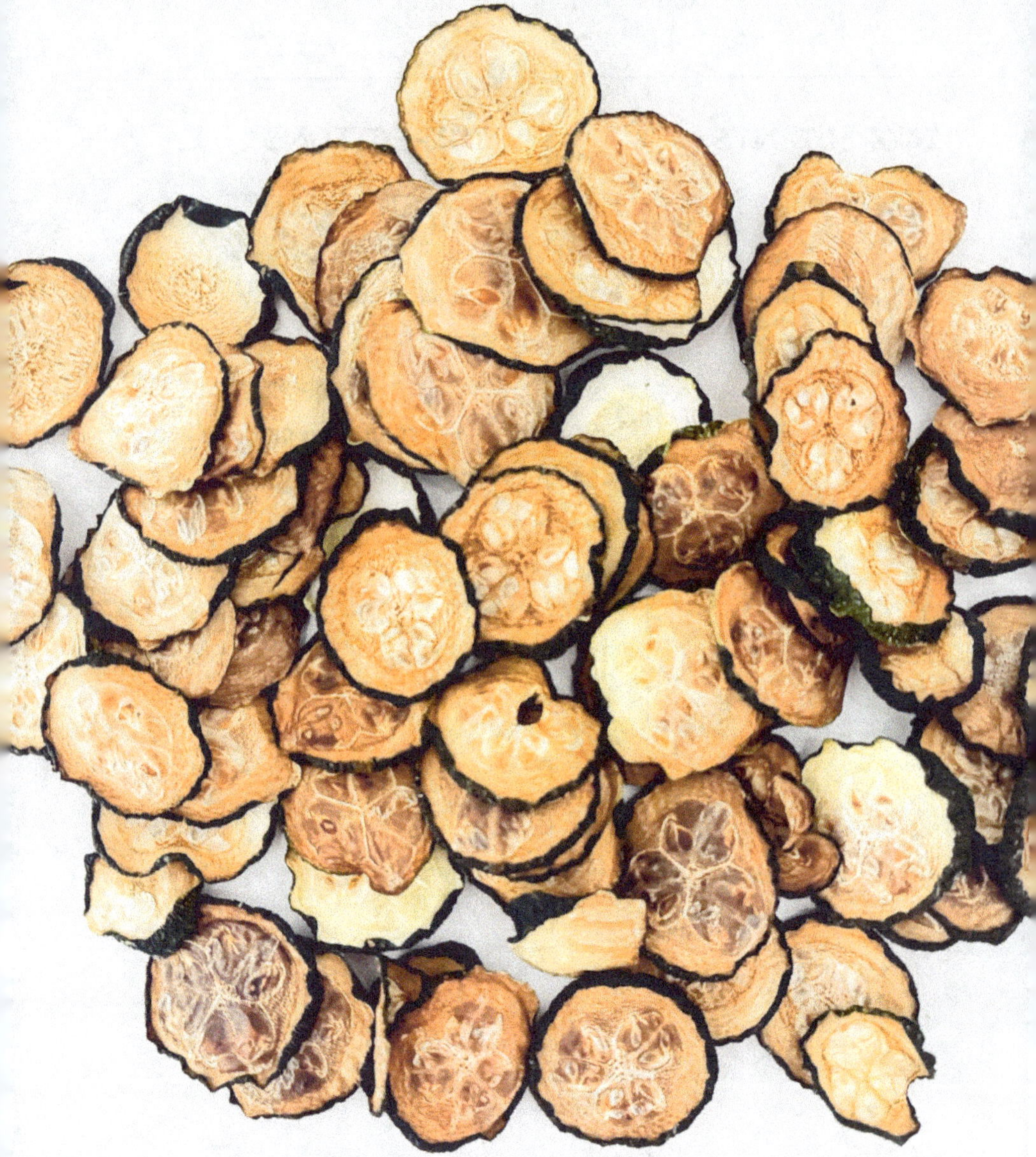

Zucchini Chips

INGREDIENTS

1 large zucchini, thinly sliced

GF DF

DIRECTIONS

1. Preheat the oven to 225°F (110°C) and line a baking sheet with parchment paper.
2. Wash and dry the zucchini. Thinly slice into even rounds and arrange them in a single layer on the prepared baking sheet.
3. Bake for 1½–2 hours, flipping halfway, or until fully dried and crisp. Cool completely before serving.
4. Store in an airtight container in the fridge for up to 14 days.

Frozen Favorites

Apple Peanut Butter Popsicles

Approximately 12 popsicles

INGREDIENTS

½ cup (125g) unsweetened applesauce

1 cup (245g) nonfat plain Greek yogurt

¼ cup (64g) unsweetened creamy peanut butter (xylitol-free)

SPECIAL TOOLS

12-cavity silicone popsicle molds & sticks

GF

DIRECTIONS

1. In a medium bowl, whisk the plain Greek yogurt, applesauce, and peanut butter until smooth and well combined.
2. Carefully pour the mixture evenly into each mold, ensuring it fills them completely. Insert the sticks and place the covers on top.
3. Freeze for 4–6 hours or until fully solid.
4. Remove the pops from the molds and serve.
5. Store in an airtight container in the freezer for up to 3 months.

Please be cautious when feeding your dog. Either remove the stick and place the ice pop in a bowl, or closely supervise to ensure they don't swallow the stick.

Banana Berry Froyo Pops

Approximately 8 popsicles

INGREDIENTS

1 ripe banana, mashed

¼ cup (37g) fresh blueberries, sliced in half

¼ cup (42g) strawberries, diced

½ cup (122g) nonfat plain Greek yogurt

SPECIAL TOOLS

8-cavity silicone popsicle molds & sticks

GF

DIRECTIONS

1. In a medium bowl, mash the banana until it's smooth. Add the plain Greek yogurt, stirring until just combined. Then, gently fold in the sliced blueberries and diced strawberries; be cautious not to break the fruit.
2. Carefully pour the mixture evenly into each mold, ensuring it fills them completely. Insert the sticks and place the covers on top.
3. Freeze for 4–6 hours or until fully solid.
4. Remove the pops from the molds and serve.
5. Store in an airtight container in the freezer for up to 3 months.

Please be cautious when feeding your dog. Either remove the stick and place the ice pop in a bowl, or closely supervise to ensure they don't swallow the stick.

Banana Split Pops

Approximately 4 popsicles

INGREDIENTS

4 small banana slices
nonfat plain Greek yogurt
¼ cup (64g) unsweetened creamy peanut butter (xylitol-free)
1 teaspoon pure honey

SPECIAL TOOLS

4-cavity silicone popsicle molds & sticks

GF

DIRECTIONS

1. Scoop the yogurt into each mold until it's about half full. Place a slice of banana on top of each and add more yogurt to fill the molds.
2. In a small heatproof bowl, mix the peanut butter and honey. Microwave on high for 20 seconds, then whisk to combine. Drizzle or spread the mixture over each mold. Insert the sticks and place the covers on top.
3. Freeze for 4–6 hours or until fully solid.
4. Remove the pops from the molds and serve.
5. Store in an airtight container in the freezer for up to 3 months.

Please be cautious when feeding your dog. Either remove the stick and place the ice pop in a bowl, or closely supervise to ensure they don't swallow the stick.

Peanut Butter Pops

Spoon unsweetened creamy peanut butter (xylitol-free) into the molds. Insert the sticks and place the covers on top. Freeze until solid for a refreshing treat.

SPECIAL TOOLS

silicone popsicle molds & sticks

GF DF

Please be cautious when feeding your dog. Either remove the stick and place the ice pop in a bowl, or closely supervise to ensure they don't swallow the stick.

Pumpkin Pops

Spoon unsweetened pumpkin purée into the molds. Insert the sticks and place the covers on top. Freeze until solid for a refreshing treat.

SPECIAL TOOLS

silicone popsicle molds & sticks

GF DF

Please be cautious when feeding your dog. Either remove the stick and place the ice pop in a bowl, or closely supervise to ensure they don't swallow the stick.

Yogurt Pops

Spoon nonfat plain Greek yogurt into the molds. Insert the sticks and place the covers on top. Freeze until solid for a refreshing treat.

SPECIAL TOOLS

silicone popsicle molds & sticks

GF

Please be cautious when feeding your dog. Either remove the stick and place the ice pop in a bowl, or closely supervise to ensure they don't swallow the stick.

Frozen Banana

Peel the banana, then wrap it in tin foil.
Freeze until solid for a refreshing treat.

GF DF

Special Occasion Delights

Apple Cupcakes

Approximately 24 mini cupcakes

INGREDIENTS

½ cup (122g) nonfat plain Greek yogurt
1 tablespoon pure maple syrup
1 cup (250g) unsweetened applesauce
1 large egg
1½ tablespoons coconut oil, melted
1¾ cups (158g) oat flour
1 teaspoon baking powder

ICING

2 ounces (56g) low-fat cream cheese
1 tablespoon pure honey
¼ cup (32g) Fuji apple slices for garnish

SPECIAL TOOLS

24-cavity mini silicone cupcake pans

GF

DIRECTIONS

1. Preheat the oven to 375°F (190°C). Use mini silicone cupcake pans or lightly coat non-silicone pans with nonstick baking spray.
2. In a large bowl, mix the plain yogurt, maple syrup, applesauce, egg, and melted coconut oil until smooth. Slowly add the oat flour and baking powder, stirring until just combined..
3. If using silicone, spoon the batter directly into the pans, filling completely. For non-silicone pans, fill each about three-quarters full.
4. Bake for 17–20 minutes or until a toothpick inserted into the center comes out clean. Let the cakes cool in the pan for 5 minutes, then carefully unmold and transfer them to a wire rack to cool completely before icing.
5. **Make the icing:** In a heatproof bowl, microwave the cream cheese and honey for 20 seconds, then whisk until smooth. If the icing is too thick, microwave for an additional 10 seconds.
6. Spread the icing on the cooled cakes and top with an apple slice for a finishing touch. (See how to frost and ice on page 113.)
7. Store in an airtight container in the fridge for up to 5 days.

Banana Pancakes

Approximately 4 pancakes

INGREDIENTS

1 ripe banana, mashed

1 egg

½ cup (60g) whole wheat flour

¼ cup low-fat Lactaid milk

DIRECTIONS

1. In a medium bowl, mash the banana until it's smooth. Add the egg, whole wheat flour, and Lactaid milk, mixing until thoroughly blended.
2. Heat a non-stick skillet over medium heat until it is hot. Pour small portions of batter into the skillet to create pancakes. Once the bubbles form, flip and cook for an additional 30 seconds to 1 minute.
3. Cool completely before serving. Storage is not recommended.

Blueberry Muffins

Approximately 24 mini muffins

INGREDIENTS

2 ripe bananas, mashed

½ cup (125g) unsweetened applesauce

1 large egg

1 tablespoon coconut oil, melted

½ cup (74g) fresh blueberries

1 cup (90g) oat flour

½ cup (48g) rolled oats

1 tablespoon baking powder

SPECIAL TOOLS

24-cavity mini silicone muffin pans

GF DF

DIRECTIONS

1. Preheat the oven to 350°F (180°C). Use mini silicone muffin pans or coat non-silicone pans with nonstick baking spray.
2. In a large bowl, mix the applesauce, melted coconut oil, egg, and bananas until smooth. Gradually add the baking soda, rolled oats, and oat flour, stirring until just combined. Gently fold in the blueberries.
3. If using silicone, spoon the batter directly into the pans, filling completely. For non-silicone pans, fill each about three-quarters full.
4. Bake for 12–15 minutes or until a toothpick inserted into the center comes out clean. Let the muffins cool in the pan for 5 minutes, then carefully unmold and transfer them to a wire rack to cool completely before serving.
5. Store in an airtight container in the fridge for up to 5 days.

Carob Brownies

Approximately 15-20 brownies

INGREDIENTS

⅓ cup (28g) carob powder (safe chocolate substitute for dogs)
½ cup (125g) unsweetened applesauce
2–3 tablespoons unsweetened coconut milk
¼ cup (64g) unsweetened almond butter
1 large egg
½ cup (45g) oat flour
¼ teaspoon baking powder
¼ cup (56g) carob chips

GF DF

DIRECTIONS

1. Preheat the oven to 325°F (165°C) and coat a 9x9-inch baking pan with nonstick baking spray.
2. In a large bowl, mix the applesauce, coconut milk, almond butter, and egg until smooth. Gradually add the carob powder, oat flour, and baking powder, stirring until just blended. Gently fold in the carob chips.
3. Spread the mixture with a spatula into the prepared baking pan, smoothing it into an even layer, pressing down firmly to flatten.
4. Bake for 12–15 minutes, or until the center is slightly soft and the edges are set. Let the brownies cool in the pan before slicing to maintain their shape and texture.
5. Store in an airtight container in the fridge for up to 5 days.

Georgia

Carrot Cake

Approximately 6–8 slices

INGREDIENTS

1 cup (110g) carrots, grated
½ cup (125g) unsweetened applesauce
¼ cup (64g) unsweetened creamy peanut butter (xylitol-free)
2 large eggs
1 cup (90g) oat flour
1 teaspoon baking powder
¼ cup water, optional to adjust batter consistency

FROSTING

¼ cup (61g) nonfat plain Greek yogurt
1 tablespoon unsweetened creamy peanut butter (xylitol-free)

SPECIAL TOOLS

6-inch round cake pan

DIRECTIONS

1. Preheat the oven to 350°F (180°C) and lightly coat a 6-inch round cake pan with nonstick baking spray.
2. In a large bowl, mix the grated carrots, apple sauce, eggs, and peanut butter thoroughly. Gradually add the oat flour and baking soda, stirring until just blended. If the batter is too thick, add water 1 tablespoon at a time.
3. Pour the batter into the prepared cake pan and smooth the surface with a spatula.
4. Bake for 20–25 minutes or until a toothpick inserted into the center comes out clean. Let the cake cool in the pan for 5 minutes, then carefully unmold and transfer to a wire rack to cool completely before frosting.
5. **Make the frosting:** In a small bowl, mix the plain Greek yogurt and peanut butter until smooth and creamy.
6. Spread the frosting on the cooled cake. (See how to frost and ice on page 113.)
7. Store in an airtight container in the fridge for up to 5 days.

Carrot Cheesecake Donuts

Approximately 24 mini donuts

INGREDIENTS

½ cup (55g) carrots, finely grated
¼ cup (63g) unsweetened applesauce
2 large eggs
2 tablespoons low-fat softened cream cheese
½ teaspoon cinnamon
1 teaspoon baking soda
1 cup (90g) oat flour

FROSTING

1 tablespoon nonfat plain Greek yogurt
4 ounces (112g) low-fat softened cream cheese
1 teaspoon pure honey
2 tablespoons low-sodium shredded cheddar cheese

SPECIAL TOOLS

24-cavity mini silicone donut pans

GF

DIRECTIONS

1. Preheat the oven to 350°F (180°C). Use mini silicone donut pans or coat non-silicone pans with nonstick baking spray.
2. In a large bowl, mix the grated carrots, applesauce, eggs, and cream cheese thoroughly. Gradually add the cinnamon, baking soda, and oat flour, stirring until just blended.
3. If using silicone, spoon the batter directly into the pans, filling completely. For non-silicone pans, fill each about three-quarters full.
4. Bake for 15–18 minutes or until a toothpick inserted into the center comes out clean. Let the donuts cool in the pan for 5 minutes, then carefully unmold and transfer them to a wire rack to cool completely before frosting.
5. **Make the frosting:** In a small bowl, mix the plain Greek yogurt, cream cheese, and honey until smooth and creamy. Gently incorporate the shredded cheddar cheese, ensuring the pieces remain visible.
6. Spread the frosting on the cooled donuts. (See how to frost and ice on page 113.)
7. Store in an airtight container in the fridge for up to 5 days.

Greek Yogurt & Fruit Bowl

Individual serving

INGREDIENTS

¼ cup (61g) nonfat plain Greek yogurt
¼ cup (37g) fresh blueberries
¼ cup (42g) strawberries, sliced
¼ banana, sliced
1 tablespoon rolled oats

GF

DIRECTIONS

1. In a small bowl, add the rolled oats and cover them with either water or nonfat plain Greek yogurt. Allow them to soak for 5–10 minutes until softened. Meanwhile, slice the banana and strawberries.
2. In a serving bowl, combine the soaked rolled oats, plain Greek yogurt, blueberries, sliced strawberries, and sliced banana. Mix gently and serve right away.
3. Not recommended for storage. Best served fresh.

Nutty Banana Mini Donuts

Approximately 12 mini donuts

INGREDIENTS

1 large ripe banana, mashed
1 tablespoon pure honey
¼ cup olive oil
1 tablespoon coconut oil, melted
1 large egg
1 tablespoon ground flax seeds
1 cup (90g) oat flour
1 teaspoon baking powder

ICING

¼ cup (64g) unsweetened almond butter
1 tablespoon unsweetened creamy peanut butter (xylitol-free)
1 teaspoon pure maple syrup
¼ cup (25g) unsalted peanuts, finely chopped for garnish

SPECIAL TOOLS

12-cavity mini silicone donut pans

GF DF

DIRECTIONS

1. Preheat the oven to 375°F (190°C). Use mini silicone donut pans or coat non-silicone pans with nonstick baking spray.
2. In a large bowl, mix the melted coconut oil, mashed banana, egg, honey, and olive oil until smooth. Gradually add the ground flax seeds, oat flour, and baking powder, stirring until just blended.
3. If using silicone, spoon the batter directly into the pans, filling completely. For non-silicone pans, fill each about three-quarters full.
4. Bake for 11–15 minutes or until a toothpick inserted into the center comes out clean. Let the donuts cool in the pan for 5 minutes, then carefully unmold and transfer them to a wire rack to cool completely before icing.
5. **Make the icing:** In a small heatproof bowl, microwave the almond butter, peanut butter, and maple syrup for 20 seconds, then whisk until smooth. If the icing is too thick, microwave for an additional 10 seconds.
6. Spread the icing on the cooled donuts and sprinkle with chopped peanuts for a finishing touch. (See how to frost and ice on page 113.)
7. Store in an airtight container in the fridge for up to 5 days.

Pumpkin Maple Mini Donuts

Approximately 24 mini donuts

INGREDIENTS

1 cup (244g) canned unsweetened pumpkin purée plus a little extra for garnish
¼ cup (63g) unsweetened applesauce
2 tablespoons pure maple syrup
2 large eggs
¼ cup olive oil
1½ cups (180g) whole wheat flour
½ teaspoon ground cinnamon
1 teaspoon baking powder

FROSTING

6 oz (168g) low-fat softened cream cheese
1 tablespoon oat flour
1 tablespoon pure honey

SPECIAL TOOLS

24-cavity mini silicone donut pans

DIRECTIONS

1. Preheat the oven to 325°F (165°C). Use mini silicone donut pans or coat non-silicone pans with nonstick baking spray.
2. In a large bowl, combine the pumpkin purée, applesauce, maple syrup, eggs, and olive oil until smooth. Gradually add the whole wheat flour, baking powder, and cinnamon, stirring until just blended.
3. If using silicone, spoon the batter directly into the pans, filling completely. For non-silicone pans, fill each about three-quarters full.
4. Bake for 16–19 minutes,or until a toothpick inserted into the center comes out clean. Let the donuts cool in the pan for 5 minutes, then carefully unmold and transfer them to a wire rack to cool completely before frosting.
5. **Make the frosting:** In a small bowl, beat the cream cheese, honey, and oat flour until well blended and smooth
6. Spread the frosting on the cooled donuts and add a dollop of pumpkin purée as a finishing touch. (See how to frost and ice on page 113.)
7. Store in an airtight container in the fridge for up to 5 days.

Spinach Scrambled Eggs

Approximately 2 servings

INGREDIENTS

2 eggs

¼ cup (7g) fresh spinach, chopped

1 teaspoon olive oil

GF DF

DIRECTIONS

1. In a non-stick skillet, heat the olive oil over medium heat. Add the chopped spinach and sauté until wilted.
2. In a bowl, whisk the eggs, then pour them into the skillet. Stir gently until scrambled and cooked through. Cool completely before serving.
3. Storage is not recommended.

Sweet Potato Egg Bowl

Approximately 2 servings

INGREDIENTS

½ cup (120g) sweet potatoes, mashed and cooked

2 large eggs

1 teaspoon olive oil

1 tablespoon nonfat plain Greek yogurt

GF DF

DIRECTIONS

1. Peel and dice the sweet potato into small cubes. Boil for 10–15 minutes until tender. Then, mash and set aside.
2. Heat the olive oil in a non-stick skillet over medium heat. Whisk the eggs in a bowl and pour them into the skillet. Stir until scrambled and cooked through.
3. In a medium bowl, mix the scrambled eggs with the mashed sweet potatoes until well combined. Let the mixture cool, then top with a dollop of nonfat plain Greek yogurt. Cool completely before serving.
4. Storage is not recommended.

Ingredient Preparation Tips

HELPFUL TIPS FOR PREPARING INGREDIENTS

How to Grind Chicken Breast Using a Food Processor or Without Special Equipment

Using a food processor: Cut the raw chicken breasts into small chunks. Place them in the processor and pulse in short bursts until finely ground. Avoid over-processing to reduce the risk of a paste-like consistency.
Without special equipment: Use a sharp knife to finely mince the chicken on a cutting board, chopping it repeatedly until you reach the desired thickness.

How to Use a Meat Thermometer

Place the thermometer in the most substantial section of the meat, avoiding contact with bone or fat. Wait a few seconds for the reading to stabilize. For ground meat, check multiple spots.

Tips for Even Cooking

Cut ingredients into consistent sizes.
Do not overcrowd pans. Leave space for heat to circulate.
Stir or flip food halfway through cooking.
Preheat your oven or pan to guarantee even heat distribution.

Safe Cooking Tips

Always verify that your cutting board and tools are properly sanitized to prevent cross-contamination.
Always use a meat thermometer to ensure risk-free cooking.
Poultry (chicken, turkey) should be cooked to 165°F (74°C).
Beef, lamb, and pork should reach 160°F (71°C).

How to Use a Cookie Stamp

Roll and shape the dough. Form the dough into symmetrical rounds and flatten each one with your hand. Gently press each round down to create a reliable surface for stamping.

Stamp the dough. Lightly flour the cookie stamp to prevent sticking. Press the stamp firmly and steadily onto the dough, then lift it straight up to view the design.

Trim with a cookie cutter. Use a round cookie cutter that is slightly larger than the stamped dough to cut around it. This step removes the excess dough while preserving the pattern.

Bake the cookies. Transfer the neatly outlined cookies to a baking sheet and bake as directed. This method ensures crisp, clean edges, avoiding the need for additional shaping after cooking.

How to Frost and Ice

Cool completely. Baked goods should be fully cooled before frosting to stop the icing from melting and sliding off.

Use the appropriate tools. A small butter knife or offset spatula offers a smooth and balanced application.

Apply with steady pressure. Use soft, controlled strokes to ensure even coverage without tearing the baked goods. Gradually add more frosting rather than piling on too much at once.

Spread evenly. Glide the frosting in light, sweeping motions, working from the center outward for a level coat.

How to Melt Carob Without a Double Boiler

Place the carob chips in a heat-safe bowl. Set the bowl over a pot of simmering water, making sure the bottom does not touch the water. Stir continuously until melted. Alternatively, microwave in 15-second intervals, stirring between each, until fully softened. Watch closely, as it can burn quickly!

How to Roll Out Dough Without a Mess

Place the dough between two sheets of parchment paper, one underneath and one on top. Roll it out to your preferred thickness with a rolling pin. This technique stops the dough from sticking and reduces the need for extra flour while keeping your workspace tidy.

Favorite Brands & Resources

Love Beets Organic Cooked Beets

When a recipe calls for beets (steamed or roasted), you can prepare them raw at home or save time by using pre-cooked beets. I suggest Love Beets—they are conveniently steamed, peeled, and ready to use with no added ingredients. Love Beets delivers the same fresh taste and texture, making meal prep quick and simple without sacrificing quality.

Crazy Richard's Creamy Natural Peanut Butter

When choosing peanut butter for recipes, select a pure variety with no added sugar, oil, salt, or harmful ingredients. I recommend Crazy Richard's Peanut Butter—made solely from peanuts and free from xylitol—making it ideal for dog-friendly recipes. Its creamy texture blends easily into batters, doughs, and frostings, ensuring excellent results every time.

A Few Other Favorites

Applegate Organics® Uncured Turkey Bacon
Crazy Richard's® Creamy Natural Almond Butter
FAGE® Total 0% Plain Greek yogurt
Fuji Apples
LACTAID® Low-fat 1% Lactose-Free Milk
Let's Do Organic® Unsweetened Shredded Coconut

To view our featured baking tools, food brands, and products, follow us on Instagram at @georgiadoodlelife. Click the Linktree in our bio to explore "Georgia's Amazon Favorites," which includes our curated "Pup Chef Pantry Favorites" for Georgia's favorite ingredients and "Pup Chef Tools & Supplies" for kitchen essentials. Please note, as an Amazon Associate, we earn from qualifying purchases.

Ingredients that Nourish

A

Almond butter is nutritious, rich in healthy fats, vitamin E, protein, and fiber, supporting skin, coat, and health. **Feed in moderation due to high calories and potential allergy risk.**

Almond flour is gluten-free, rich in healthy fats, protein, and fiber, supporting muscle and digestion. **Feed in moderation due to density and calories—choose unsweetened varieties.**

Apples are a crunchy, low-calorie snack rich in fiber and vitamin C, promoting dental health and digestion.

Applesauce offers fiber and vitamin C, supporting digestive health. **Choose unsweetened varieties with no added sugar.**

Asparagus is rich in folic acid and vitamins A and C. It supports immune health, cell growth, and vision. Its fiber helps with digestion and may reduce blood pressure.

B

Bananas increase energy, aid digestion, and promote heart health because they contain high levels of potassium, fiber, vitamin B6, and vitamin C. **Feed in moderation—consuming too many can cause constipation or elevate blood sugar.**

Beef is a good source of protein that supports muscle health and supplies amino acids for energy, tissue repair, and immune function. **Choose ground beef that is at least 90% lean and unseasoned.**

Beets are high in antioxidants, fiber, and essential minerals, including folate, which boost immune health and overall vitality.

Bell peppers are rich in vitamins A and C, which support eye health and strengthen the immune system. Their antioxidant qualities help combat oxidative stress, while their fiber promotes healthy digestion.

Blackberries are high in fiber, vitamin C, and antioxidants, which support immune health, digestion, and reduce inflammation. **Feed in moderation and monitor for upset stomachs.**

Blueberries contain high levels of antioxidants, fiber, and vitamins C and K. They support the immune system, improve brain function, and promote overall health. **Introduce them gradually to assess tolerance.**

Broccoli has vitamins C and K, fiber, and antioxidants that support immunity, aid digestion, and reduce inflammation. **Consuming too much may lead to gas or stomach discomfort.**

Butternut squash is packed with vitamins A and C, crucial for maintaining healthy skin, good eyesight, and boosting the immune system. Its high fiber content also aids digestion.

C

Cabbage is a great source of vitamins C and K, which are essential for immune health and blood clotting. Its fiber supports digestion, and its antioxidants may reduce inflammation. **Introduce it gradually to prevent digestive discomfort.**

Cantaloupe is low in calories, has a high water content, and is very hydrating. It is also rich in vitamins A and C. **Feed in moderation due to its natural sugar content.**

Carob powder and chips are a safe alternative to chocolate. They are rich in vitamins and antioxidants and naturally have a sweet flavor. **Feed in moderation due to their richness and potential to cause digestive upset.**

Carrots are rich in beta-carotene, fiber, and essential vitamins, which support healthy vision, aid digestion, and boost the immune system.

Cauliflower is low in calories and high in fiber. It offers vitamins C, K, and B6, which support heart health, immune function, and overall well-being. **Introduce slowly to avoid digestive upset.**

Celery is low in calories, high in water, and helps hydrate dogs. It provides vitamins A, C, and K, and its crunch helps clean teeth.

Cheese provides calcium for strong bones and teeth, as well as protein for muscle support. **Serve in moderation and choose low-sodium varieties. Avoid those with added flavors or herbs.**

Chicken is an excellent source of high-quality protein that supports muscle health, increases energy, and enhances immune function. **Serve cooked, boneless, skinless chicken breast without seasoning.**

Chicken broth enhances flavor while providing hydration and essential minerals such as potassium, which aids in joint health and helps maintain proper fluid balance. **Use only low-sodium varieties with no artificial additives.**

Cinnamon, in small amounts, helps reduce inflammation, controls blood sugar levels, and provides antioxidants to support overall health. **Do not use cassia—use only plain Ceylon. Use sparingly.**

Coconut flour is a gluten-free, nutrient-rich flour that's high in fiber. It helps regulate blood sugar, supports digestion, and promotes healthy skin and coat. **Use it sparingly since it absorbs a lot of moisture.**

Coconut milk has healthy fats that provide energy and aid in nutrient absorption. It also offers vitamins C and E, known for their antioxidant benefits. **Always opt for unsweetened varieties.**

Coconut oil offers healthy fats that enhance coat shine and support joint health. **Introduce gradually and feed in moderation to prevent gastrointestinal upset.**

Cranberries are rich in antioxidants and vitamin C, which strengthen immunity, decrease inflammation, and promote urinary and digestive health. **Serve fresh without added sugar.**

Cream cheese is rich in calcium and vitamin A, supporting bones and vision. Opt for plain, low-fat varieties without added flavors. **Feed in moderation because of its high fat content.**

Cucumbers are a low-calorie snack rich in vitamins K and C, essential for healthy skin and bones. **Serve only seedless varieties and peel to prevent digestive issues.**

E

Eggs provide a rich source of protein that supports muscle growth, enhances coat shine, and boosts energy levels.

F

Flax seeds are high in omega-3 fatty acids, supporting healthy skin, coat, and joint function, while also providing fiber for digestive health. **Feed in moderation to avoid digestive upset.**

G

Green beans are a low-calorie snack packed with fiber and vitamins C and K, which support digestion and promote strong bones.

Greek yogurt has probiotics that support gut health and digestion. It provides calcium and protein to support strong bones, teeth, and muscles. **Serve plain, low-fat, or fat-free.**

H

Honey is a natural sweetener that provides energy, antioxidants, and aids digestion. **It's not suitable for puppies under one year old. Choose 100% pure honey only. Use it sparingly because it's high in calories and natural sugars.**

K

Kiwis are rich in vitamin C and fiber, which boost immune function and aid digestion. Their antioxidants help improve skin health and may lower blood pressure. **Feed in small amounts due to their natural sugar content.**

M

Mangos are rich in vitamins A, C, and E, which support skin, immunity, and overall health. **Feed in moderation due to the high sugar content.**

Maple syrup is a natural sweetener rich in antioxidants and minerals like manganese and zinc that support metabolism, energy, and immunity. **Use sparingly—opt for 100% pure.**

Milk provides calcium for strong bones and teeth. Some dogs are lactose intolerant, **so use in small amounts or opt for Lactaid, low-fat goat's milk, or unsweetened coconut milk.**

O

Oat flour is a gluten-free, fiber-rich option that supports digestion and helps sustain energy. **Feed in moderation and introduce gradually to avoid digestive upset.**

Olive oil provides healthy fats, including omega-3 fatty acids, which support healthy skin, coats, and joints. **Use extra-virgin olive oil sparingly to minimize excess fat.**

Oranges are rich in vitamin C, boost the immune system, and support skin health. Their fiber content promotes digestion. **Feed in moderation due to acidity and sugar content.**

P

Papayas are rich in vitamins A and C, which support eye health and immune function. Their enzymes aid in digestion, and antioxidants may help reduce inflammation.

Peaches are rich in fiber, vitamin A, and vitamin C, all of which are essential for healthy skin and digestion. **Feed fresh in moderation.**

Peanut butter and peanuts provide protein, healthy fats, vitamin E, and magnesium for heart, muscle, and overall health. **Choose unsalted, unsweetened, and xylitol-free options, and feed in moderation due to calorie content.**

Pears are rich in fiber and vitamin C, which help support digestion and immune health. **Feed in moderation, as excessive fiber intake can cause digestive discomfort.**

Pineapples provide vitamin C and bromelain, which may aid digestion and help hydration. **Feed in moderation due to their natural sugar and acidity content.**

Plums are rich in antioxidants and fiber, helping digestion, immunity, inflammation, and heart and muscle health. **Feed in moderation due to natural sugars and laxative effects.**

Pumpkin and pumpkin purée aid digestion, relieve constipation and diarrhea, and supply beta-carotene for immune and skin health. **Feed in moderation to avoid gut imbalance.**

R

Raspberries are high in fiber and vitamin C, which support digestive and immune health. Their antioxidants help reduce inflammation. **Feed in small amounts, as they may affect blood sugar levels.**

Rolled oats provide fiber, help regulate blood sugar, and offer lasting energy, along with extra essential vitamins and minerals. **Use plain oats without added sugar or flavorings, and introduce them gradually to avoid digestive upset.**

S

Shredded coconut provides healthy fats that promote skin and coat health. **Offer in small portions. Choose unsweetened types.**

Spinach is packed with vitamins A, C, and K, iron, and antioxidants that boost immunity and health. **Feed in moderation due to a compound that may reduce nutrient absorption.**

Strawberries provide antioxidants for immunity and fiber for digestion. **Feed in moderation due to natural sugars and potential digestive issues.**

Sweet potatoes are rich in fiber and provide vitamins A, C, and B6, aiding digestion, immune health, and skin. **Serve in moderation to avoid digestive issues.**

T

Turkey is a lean protein that supports muscle health and provides energy with no extra fat. **Choose ground turkey that is at least 93% lean.**

Turkey bacon is a leaner alternative to traditional bacon, offering a source of protein and B vitamins. **Use sparingly due to its high sodium and fat content.**

W

Watermelon is a hydrating fruit packed with vitamins A, B6, and C, which support immune function and skin health. **Feed in moderation due to its high natural sugar content.**

Whole wheat flour is a rich source of fiber and essential nutrients that aid digestion and help regulate blood sugar levels. **Introduce gradually to avoid digestive upset.**

Z

Zucchini is low in calories and rich in vitamins A, C, and B6, which boost immunity, hydration, and digestion. **Feed in moderation, as it may cause stomach upset.**

Recipe List

Index

Georgia's "Paw" Of Approval

INDEX BY KEY INGREDIENTS

INDEX BY TREAT TYPE

Frozen Treats & Popsicles

Muffins

Treats

Reference Sections

Conclusion

Thank you for being a part of this adventure and sharing delightful goodies with your furry best friend! Whether it's an everyday ritual or a momentous occasion, nothing is more gratifying than watching your furry friend savor what you've made from the heart. Whipping up dog-friendly creations is a terrific way to show your pup how much they're valued while ensuring each bite is filled with wholesome goodness.

Every recipe is crafted with consideration for flavor and health. I hope these selections enrich your friendship and brighten your dog's day. While all the treats are produced with human-grade ingredients, some—primarily those without added natural sweetness—may be more pup-pleasing than people-pleasing. You'll also find plenty of snacks perfect for you and your pup to enjoy together. Remember, you don't need to be a professional chef to be a *Pup Chef*—a little effort makes a big difference, and the sparkle in their eyes says it all.

Here's to many more wagging tails, happy tummies, and precious moments with our furry best friends. Follow Georgia's adventures on Instagram @georgiadoodlelife, where our story continues.

thank
you &
acknowledgments
Georgia

This cookbook would not have been possible without the endless support and inspiration of those around me.

To my sweet Georgia, the most incredible culinary critic and the driving force behind this endeavor, thank you for being my loyal companion and helping me find solace in the simple things.

A heartfelt thank you to Scott—his influence continues to echo throughout my journey. He left an unforgettable mark on my life, and after he passed away, the emptiness without him and his beloved dog led me to adopt Georgia. She has been my source of strength, compelling me to heal and embrace what lies ahead. I know Scott would be smiling to see the love Georgia and I share and how she has empowered me to create something meaningful.

Thank you to my friends, family, and the pet community for being enthusiastic taste-testers and providing invaluable feed-back. Your generosity means more than words can express.

Thank you, dear reader, for trusting me to help you care for your furry best friend. I hope these recipes bring as much happiness to your home as they have to mine.

Finally, this book is for all the amazing dogs who show us their unwavering devotion. May you receive every treat and kindness the universe has to offer.

With gratitude,

Margot Phillips

Bonus Content

Access convenient, printable recipe cards for all your favorites from ***Pup Chef: 50 Recipes Your Furry Best Friend Will Love***. Click the links below to download the recipe cards by chapter.

- Healthy Fruit & Veggie Snacks: https://bit.ly/4j6lJ5b
- Tasty Treats: https://bit.ly/3DFRBPm
- One Ingredient Healthy Bites: https://bit.ly/4c61CSD
- Frozen Favorites: https://bit.ly/4j8j9f7
- Special Occasion Delights: https://bit.ly/43LmM6v

www.ingramcontent.com/pod-product-compliance
Lightning Source LLC
Chambersburg PA
CBHW060428130626
46555CB00005B/2270
* 9 7 9 8 9 9 8 5 0 3 8 1 8 *